Benjamin Franklin

Other Scholastic Biographies you will enjoy:

Thomas Jefferson
Man with a Vision
by Ruth Crisman

Colin Powell
A Biography
by Jim Haskins

Faithful Friend
The Story of Florence Nightingale
by Beatrice Siegel

Christopher Columbus
Admiral of the Ocean Sea
by Jim Haskins

Nelson Mandela
"No Easy Walk to Freedom"
by Barry Denenberg

Jesse Jackson
A Biography
by Patricia C. McKissack

Benjamin Franklin

Deborah Kent

SCHOLASTIC INC.
New York Toronto London Auckland Sydney

Picture Credits

Front cover courtesy of Superstock. Page 5 courtesy of the Library of Congress. Page 7 courtesy of the Bostonian Society. Pages 10, 12, 18, 52, 57, 62, 75, 114, and 117 courtesy of UPI/Bettmann. Pages 15, 24, 25, 42, 51, 106, and 119 courtesy of the Library Company of Philadelphia. Pages 29, 31, 36, 44, 88, 102, 104, and 108 courtesy of Culver Pictures. Pages 49, 68, 79, 99, and 100 courtesy of the New York Public Library. Page 60 courtesy of North Wind Picture Archives. Page 66 courtesy of The Franklin Institute. Page 82 courtesy of AP/Wide World. Page 85 courtesy of the Henry E. Huntington Library and Art Gallery. Page 93 courtesy of the Metropolitan Museum of Art.

ISBN 0-590-46012-9

12   11   10   9   8   7   6   5   4   3   2   1   3   4   5   6   7   8/9

Printed in the U.S.A.   40

First Scholastic printing, September 1993

CONTENTS

Benjamin Franklin

Prologue

Oxford University was a haven for the finest scholars of Europe. For centuries philosophers and poets, naturalists and mathematicians had walked its tree-lined paths and pored over books in its vast, ivy-covered libraries.

By the middle of the eighteenth century, no American had ever been honored by this great center of learning. To many Europeans, America was a savage wilderness, a land of famines and howling wolves. Its inhabitants must be busy just trying to survive. How could any of them find time for the life of the mind?

Yet, in a solemn ceremony in April 1762, Oxford University conferred the degree of Doctor of Civil Laws on a man from England's faraway Pennsylvania colony. He was a writer, philosopher, and scientist named Benjamin Franklin.

Benjamin Franklin was well-known to most of the people gathered at Oxford on the day he received his honorary degree. Some had corresponded with him for years, exchanging ideas about everything from ocean currents to systems of government. Many had read his articles on electricity. Nearly all of them had chuckled over his humorous letters to the editor, which appeared regularly in London newspapers.

Franklin's achievements seemed even more remarkable to the Oxford scholars because, unlike most of them, he was not born into society's upper class. He was a printer by trade. He had spent only two years attending school. He did not grow up with the privileges of wealth. But he was endowed with natural gifts that were far more valuable. Franklin possessed inexhaustible energy. He was an unquenchable optimist who could find advantages in almost any situation. And he had endless curiosity about nearly every aspect of life.

The scholars of Oxford recognized Benjamin Franklin as a man of extraordinary genius. Though more than two centuries have passed since his death, historians still consider Franklin to be one of the most brilliant human beings America has ever produced.

1
The Shop on Union Street

Perhaps if he had worked harder at his math lessons, Ben could have escaped the candle shop. His father always said he should be a minister when he grew up. That was why he was sent to school, to prepare for a life in the church.

But school was a disaster. Years later, in his autobiography, Benjamin Franklin recalled, "I acquired fair Writing pretty soon, but I fail'd in the Arithmetic and made no Progress in it." After only two years, when he was ten years old, Ben's formal education came to an end. He stayed home to help in his father's shop, making and selling soap and candles.

For endless hours, Ben sweated over great pots of boiling tallow. He cut candlewicks, filled molds to make soap, and waited on customers. But all the time he worked, his mind searched toward the future. He longed to meet people and discover a world beyond his father's shop on Union Street, even beyond the city of Boston itself.

One of Ben's older brothers, Josiah, had become a sailor. He was away from home for years at a time. When he returned, he brought tales of far-off lands and strange customs. Ben hoped maybe some day he, too, could go to sea.

After the long, dull hours in the shop, Ben looked forward to the evenings. The whole family would gather around the long supper table — Ben's father and mother, Josiah and Abiah Franklin; his uncle Benjamin, for whom he was named; and as many of his brothers and sisters as lived at home at a given time. Ben was born in 1706 and was almost the baby of the family — the fifteenth of seventeen children. He was the tenth and youngest of the boys. His father, too, was a youngest son. In fact, Ben descended from a series of youngest sons that stretched back five generations.

Josiah Franklin, Ben's father, had grown up in England. He worked there as a dyer of linen and other fine cloth. But there was little need for dyers in colonial Massachusetts. When Josiah Franklin reached New England in 1683, he could not find work in his former trade. At last he switched to candlemaking, and built up a thriving business.

Josiah Franklin married young, but his first

The house in which Benjamin Franklin was born.

wife died after giving birth to their seventh child. After her death Josiah married Abiah Folger, Ben's mother. Abiah's father, Peter Folger, was one of the first British settlers in Massachusetts. He wrote many essays on religious and political topics. Abiah's mother, however, came to the New World as a servant girl, and could neither read nor write.

Mealtimes were always lively at the home of

Josiah and Abiah Franklin. As the dishes passed back and forth, Ben listened to passionate discussions about current events. Sometimes Uncle Benjamin recited one of the poems he had written. When the table was finally cleared, Ben's father would get out his fiddle and entertain the family with some of the old songs he had learned when he was a boy.

Despite Ben's poor performance at school, Josiah Franklin was convinced that his youngest son was exceptionally talented. Ben had taught himself to read as a small child. Books were few and precious in colonial Massachusetts, but Ben read hungrily. Uncle Benjamin had brought some books with him from England, so the Franklins had a better library than most of their neighbors. In addition to collections of sermons, hymnals, and, of course, the Bible, there may have been Shakespeare's plays, works on Greek and Roman history, and books about "natural philosophy," as science was called at the time. They were nothing like the storybooks that children enjoy reading today. But Ben was enthralled. He read everything he could, and what he read, he remembered.

Josiah Franklin was appalled when Ben, his most promising son, announced his intention to become a sailor. The sea had already lured young Josiah away from home. Ben must not be allowed to follow his brother.

Ben's father began taking him on long walks

whenever business in the shop was slow. Together they explored the narrow, crooked streets of Boston. In the early 1700s, Boston had about 6,000 people, making it the largest city in the American colonies. Pigs foraged for tidbits in the gutters. Sometimes a flock of geese wandered from the grassy common, the city's central square, to honk and flap through the streets. Fancy carriages rattled over cobblestones, and

The streets of early Boston.

heavy farm wagons rumbled by, loaded with corn and potatoes and hams destined for the city market.

Soaring above the city were the steeples of eleven churches. Massachusetts had been founded nearly a century before as a haven for the Puritans, who had been persecuted in England. The early Puritans had been very strict. They wore plain dark clothes and forbade drinking and dancing. Puritanism had eased somewhat, and by now taverns were even more plentiful in Boston than churches. One historian has commented that by the time Ben was born, water was mainly used for transportation and drowning.

On their walks Josiah Franklin introduced his son to many of the city's tradesmen. Ben watched wheelwrights, carpenters, and harnessmakers at work. He saw coopers making barrels out of wooden staves, and blacksmiths shaping red-hot bars of iron. He learned how barbers treated sick people by placing leeches on their bodies to suck the illness away. When they reached Union Street once more, Ben's father would ask hopefully if he were interested in studying any of the trades they had seen.

Ben was a tireless observer, fascinated by everything around him. But none of the trades they saw appealed to him very much. Reluctantly he went back to the candle shop.

Though Ben was expected to help his father, he still had plenty of time for fun. With the other boys of the neighborhood he fished and swam and rowed on the river. One day, when he was ten, he and his friends gathered a pile of bricks from a nearby building site and constructed a pier into the middle of their favorite fishing pond. The building owner was less than pleased when he discovered their project the next morning. The boys had to undo all of their hard work and put the bricks back where they found them.

Ben went home and complained to his father. He argued that the pier had been very useful for anyone who wanted to fish. But, as he wrote in his autobiography, his father "convinced me that nothing was useful which was not honest."

Such carefree days ended abruptly when Ben was twelve years old. His father decided that the time had come for him to learn a trade that could provide him with a prosperous future. Since Ben loved books, he decided to apprentice him to his older brother James, a printer.

The conditions of apprenticeship in colonial Boston were very strict. The boys' father paid James a fee for Ben's room, board, and training. James, in his turn, promised to teach Ben all that he knew about printing books and pamphlets, newspapers and advertisements. For his part,

Ben swore to give James his unbending loyalty, to obey him, and to remain in his service for nine years — until he should reach the age of twenty-one.

James and Franklin were brothers. But under the contract that both signed in 1718, James became master, and Ben was his apprentice.

Ben Franklin working in his brother's print shop.

2
The Printer's Apprentice

Ben quickly mastered the art of setting type and printing pages on the noisy presses in James' shop. He enjoyed meeting the customers who brought in work to be printed up. It was exciting to find so many people who liked to read as much as he did himself.

Ben made friends with several apprentice booksellers, who often stopped by on errands for their masters. He persuaded them to lend him books from their masters' shops. Ben usually started reading the moment his day's work was over. He finished his book by candlelight, and returned it to the bookseller in the morning.

Soon after he became James' apprentice, Ben began writing poetry. He was very proud of his first efforts. One poem recounted the capture of the infamous pirate Blackbeard, and another was a mournful ballad about a recent shipwreck off the Massachusetts coast.

In those days, long before television and tape recordings, street vendors often sold broadsides — poems or songs printed on a single sheet of paper. These broadsides were a popular form of entertainment. James printed Ben's poems, and Ben set to work selling them on the streets.

Franklin selling his ballads in the streets of Boston.

To his delight, they sold well, especially the lament for the drowned sea captain and his daughters. He began to think that he might become a great poet.

His uncle Benjamin was thrilled. He had written poetry for years, and hoped that his namesake would follow in his footsteps. But Ben's father shook his head, and warned him that versemakers were usually beggars. Ben gave up his ambition to become a poet. Years later, looking back, he admitted that his poems had not really been very good. Unfortunately, no copies survive today, so we cannot judge for ourselves.

If he could not write poetry, he could develop his ability to communicate in prose. After the shop closed for the night, Ben settled down to a series of writing exercises. First he read a story or essay. Then he set it down in verse. Days later, he took out the verses he had written, and turned them into his own version of the original story or essay.

When Ben was sixteen, he became a vegetarian. In his writings, he explains little about his decision, but apparently it grew out of a conviction that it was morally wrong to eat the flesh of other living creatures. He soon discovered that vegetarian meals were much cheaper than meals of beef and mutton. He bought books with the money he saved, and began to build a small library of his own.

Ben was busier than ever before, but he still

found time for swimming. He discovered that he could take longer strokes when he held light wooden paddles, or *palettes*, in his hands. He also made special sandals, which enabled him to kick in the water like a frog. The palettes and the sandals for kicking were Benjamin Franklin's earliest known inventions.

Although he had plenty to do, Ben's life was a lonely one. Few of the boys his age understood his passion for reading and writing, and he did not make friends easily. Furthermore, he did not get along with James, his brother and master. They both held strong opinions, and they were often in conflict. When Ben suggested improvements in the shop, James became angry. How could a mere apprentice, and his own little brother besides, dare to tell him how to run his business!

In 1721, James Franklin and two of his friends launched a new project — a newspaper called the *New England Courant*. The *Courant* consisted of a single sheet, printed with two columns on each side. Most of the space was devoted to local news such as the arrivals and departures of ships in Boston Harbor. But to make the paper more lively, James Franklin also printed letters to the editor that expressed views on current controversies. During the long, hot summer of 1721, the most controversial topic in Boston was inoculation against smallpox.

Since its founding, Boston had suffered six

Cotton Mather was one of the most influential figures in colonial Boston.

major smallpox epidemics. Now the city reeled under yet another outbreak of this dreaded disease. One man, Cotton Mather, believed that a major epidemic could be avoided. Mather had learned about inoculation from one of his African servants. In Africa and in parts of the Near East, healthy people were deliberately infected with fluid from the rashes of people who were already sick with the disease. Most of the time, the inoculated person came down with a mild case of smallpox, and was then protected by natural immunity against developing a more severe case later on.

Cotton Mather was a scholar, a writer, and a minister of the Congregational Church. An offshoot of Puritanism, the Congregational Church set the moral tone for colonial New England. Cotton Mather and his father, the famous minister Increase Mather, were among the most influential men in Boston. When the Mathers declared that Bostonians must be inoculated, the decision carried authority.

James Franklin and his colleagues, however, had long opposed the Mathers, whose zealous preachings about sin seemed oppressive to these spirited young men. Now the *Courant* took a firm stand against inoculation. It printed warnings from leading physicians, who pointed out that some people died after being inoculated. According to the *Courant*, the practice of inoculation was nothing but an old wives' tale. Outraged, Cotton Mather dubbed the writers of the *Courant* "the Hell-Fire Club."

By the end of the summer, the epidemic ran its course. The work at the *Courant* settled into a routine. Ben often chuckled over the letters to the editor he was given to print. They were actually written by James and his friends, using such humorous pen names as Ichabod Henroost, Betty Frugal, and Tabitha Talkative. Perhaps his writing exercises had given him confidence. At any rate, Ben decided to write a few letters of his own.

Early one morning Ben crept down to the shop and slipped a sealed envelope under the door. When James arrived at work, he found a letter to the editor of the *Courant,* apparently written by a young woman who signed herself "Silence Dogood." In the months that followed, James received and printed more than a dozen of Silence Dogood's letters, which poked fun at many aspects of Boston life. In one letter, Silence took aim at Harvard College. She pointed out the foolishness of parents who sent their children in pursuit of a higher education, "insensible of the solidarity of their skulls." At Harvard, these young people learned "little more than to carry themselves handsomely . . . (which might as well be acquired in a dancing-school.)" In another letter, Silence lampooned popular broadsides. She quoted one such poem, supposedly written on the death of a loving wife:

She kissed her husband some little time
before she expired,
Then leaned her head the pillow on, just
out of breath and tired.

James Franklin and his friends spent hours trying to guess who was writing the Silence Dogood letters. No one suspected Ben, the sixteen-year-old apprentice. Ben listened to their wild speculations, and kept his secret.

James soon had other problems to distract him. Pirates had been marauding the coast, and the Massachusetts government had done little to protect the colony. One issue of the *Courant* criticized the government's inaction. The Mathers, still seething over the inoculation debate, used their influence to have James thrown into jail. While

Pirates threatened the safety of ships along the coast of New England.

his brother sat in prison, Ben had complete charge of the newspaper.

James was released after a month, but the feud did not end there. In January 1723, James wrote in the *Courant*, "There are many persons who seem to be more than ordinary religious, but yet are on several accounts worse by far than those who pretend to no religion at all." By today's standards, such an editorial comment seems mild. But to the Mathers, this was the final insult. The governing council of Boston forbade James from publishing the *Courant* any longer. To save the paper, James and his friends decided to put it in Ben's name. Since an apprentice could not run a newspaper, James canceled Ben's apprenticeship contract. However, he drew up another contract in secret, which Ben was obliged to sign.

The arrangement was uncomfortable for both James and Ben. James felt threatened by his talented younger brother, who seemed on the brink of taking over his whole printing business. When Ben finally admitted that he had written the Silence Dogood letters, James was even more upset. Proud of his accomplishments, Ben did not make the situation any easier. Later he wrote that his arrogant behavior during those trying months was "one of the first errata of my life."

Finally Ben made up his mind to look for work somewhere else. Legally he was still an apprentice, bound to James until he should turn twenty-one. If he ran away, he would be breaking the law. But in order to prosecute him, James would have to admit that his apprentice had been running the newspaper.

As Ben expected, James did not reveal their secret contract. But when he realized that Ben wanted to leave, he warned the city's other printers not to hire him. Eager to avoid trouble, they were willing to follow his wishes. If Ben hoped to strike out on his own, he would have to leave Boston, the only home he had ever known.

3
The Journey to Philadelphia

By selling some of his precious books, Ben paid for passage on a sloop bound for New York. He made his plans in secret, knowing that he could be arrested for breaking his apprenticeship contract. In September 1723, like an escaping criminal, he slipped away from Boston.

During the voyage, the ship was becalmed off Block Island, and some of the sailors fished for cod over the side. Ben was still a vegetarian, but the fish smelled delicious when it was served hot from the frying pan. For a few minutes Ben struggled, telling himself that this was the murder of creatures that had not injured any of the men. Then he remembered that, when the fish were being cleaned, he had seen the remains of smaller fish in their bellies. He concluded that if the fish ate one another, why couldn't people eat them? "So convenient a thing it is to be a *reasonable* Creature," he commented in his autobiography, "since it enables one to find or make a Reason for every thing one has a mind to do."

Friendless and alone, Ben reached New York after three days at sea. He soon discovered that the city was smaller than Boston. It had no newspaper, and only one printer, William Bradford. Bradford did not need an assistant. But, he explained kindly, his son had just established a printing business in Philadelphia. Perhaps he could use an extra hand.

Ben's reception in New York must have been discouraging. But he did not retreat back to Boston. Instead, he headed for Philadelphia to look for work with William Bradford's son.

On the first leg of the journey, Ben set out by ship from New York to Perth Amboy, New Jersey. The trip across Staten Island Bay should have taken only a few hours. But almost as soon as the ship left port, a fierce squall blew up. Water sloshed across the deck, and the wind tore the sails to pieces. As the battered ship tossed helplessly on the waves, a drunken passenger slipped overboard. Before the man's head could disappear beneath the surface, Ben seized him by the hair and hauled him back to safety.

They finally landed in Perth Amboy, after thirty

22

hours of hard sailing. Exhausted, soaked to the skin, and feverish, Ben found an inn and collapsed into bed. By the next morning he had recovered, but he realized that his money was running low. Instead of paying to ride in a coach, he decided to cross New Jersey on foot. He covered the fifty miles from Perth Amboy to Burlington in two days, walking or occasionally hitching a ride on a farmer's wagon. By now he was beginning to wish he had never left Boston after all. He was so dirty and bedraggled that he wondered if anyone would consider hiring him.

At Burlington, Ben hoped to catch a boat that would take him down the Delaware River to Philadelphia. When he finally reached the docks, he learned that the regular passenger boat would not leave for three more days. Later that afternoon, however, he saw a small craft loading up, and joined its passengers and crew. They set out in the evening and, after rowing most of the night, reached Philadelphia's Market Street wharf at about nine o'clock on a Sunday morning.

Benjamin Franklin arrived in Philadelphia tired, ragged, and almost out of money. His pockets were stuffed with the few extra socks and shirts he had carried with him. Above all, he was hungry. As he walked up the street, he spotted a boy carrying a loaf of bread. Half starved as he was, Ben thought it looked delicious. He asked the boy where he had bought it and headed for the bakery he described.

The waterfront in colonial Philadelphia.

At the bakery, Ben asked for a few biscuits — the sort of cheap loaves he had often eaten in Boston. But the baker had never heard of them. Ben asked for a three-penny loaf, but again was told that the baker had no such thing. At last Ben simply handed over three pennies and asked for as much bread as they could buy. The baker handed him three enormous puffy rolls.

Ben left the shop and set off down Market

An early engraving of downtown Philadelphia.

Street. As he walked along, a girl named Deborah Read watched him from her doorway. She saw a sturdy, broad-shouldered boy of seventeen, his light brown hair tousled, his clothes wrinkled and dirty, his pockets bulging. He munched a huge, floury roll, and carried two more, one tucked under each arm. He looked so ridiculous that she burst out laughing. Years later, Deborah Read would become Benjamin Franklin's wife.

25

More than a century later, an American artist named David Rent Etter painted a picture of Benjamin Franklin, clutching his fresh rolls, on his first morning in the city that was to become his home. The picture has become part of American folklore. It symbolizes Benjamin Franklin's humble beginnings, from which he rose to become one of the most prominent men in colonial America.

4
The City of Brotherly Love

Philadelphia in 1723 was almost as large as Boston, but the two cities were very different. Already Boston had stood for nearly a century. Three generations of English immigrants had grown up on its crowded streets. It had been founded by the Puritans, with their strict notions about evil and righteousness, and it was not a city which welcomed new ideas.

Philadelphia, on the other hand, had been established only forty years before. Its founder was an English Quaker named William Penn. Like the Puritans of Massachusetts, the Quakers had fled England in search of religious freedom. But unlike the Puritans, they wanted freedom of worship for all, not only for those who shared their beliefs.

In the Pennsylvania colony, William Penn tried to create a haven where people of diverse backgrounds could live together in peace. For this reason he named its leading city *Philadelphia*, from the Greek word meaning "city of brotherly love."

Philadelphia was new, energetic, and growing day by day. Its citizens were an assorted cast of newcomers from England, Scotland, Ireland, and many of the German provinces. In fact, so many Germans lived in Pennsylvania that some predicted English would become a second language.

Much of the land around Philadelphia was under cultivation. Pennsylvania was already known as the breadbasket of the colonies, its fertile soil producing enormous crops of corn and wheat. But a few miles out of the city, a traveler could be surrounded by dense forests. The American frontier stretched endlessly to the west, and all of that land seemed to beg for European settlement. For hundreds of families seeking to carve a new life from the wilderness, Philadelphia was the last outpost of civilization.

Philadelphia was the perfect setting for Benjamin Franklin. Almost by chance he found himself in a place where his genius could develop and flourish. Like the rough frame of a new house, Philadelphia waited for the architect who would give it unique character.

The morning after he reached the city, Benjamin Franklin searched out William Bradford's son. Andrew Bradford had no work for the eager young man. But he suggested that Franklin try the shop of another printer, Samuel Keimer.

Franklin was unimpressed by Keimer's shop. The equipment was old and in poor repair, and Keimer himself seemed silly and eccentric. But Bradford and Keimer were the only printers in Philadelphia. When Keimer offered him a job, Franklin was happy to accept.

Within a few days, Franklin moved into a boardinghouse run by a widow named Mrs. Read. By chance she was the mother of Deborah Read,

Deborah Read, who would later become Franklin's wife.

the girl who had laughed when she saw him on his first morning in Philadelphia. Deborah was a plain, quiet young woman, but she was soon charmed by the burly young man with the ready smile. They spent many pleasant evenings talking together in the Reads' parlor.

When he wrote about his years in Boston, Benjamin Franklin always described his rigorous studies. But when he wrote about his first winter in Philadelphia, his accounts were also about new friends. He had money in his pockets, and he could come and go as he pleased. Besides Deborah, he soon met many other "young people of the town, that were lovers of reading, with whom I spent my evenings very pleasantly."

As he threw himself into his glorious new life, Franklin tried to put memories of Boston behind him. He did not even write to his family to say where he was. But his brother-in-law, a ship's captain named Robert Holmes, often docked at the nearby port of New Castle, Delaware. On one visit, Holmes heard about Philadelphia's new young printer, and realized he had located his long-lost relative. Immediately he wrote to Franklin, urging him to return to his worried family. Franklin answered with a letter explaining why he had left Boston and listing his reasons for staying away.

When Holmes received the letter, he happened to be with Sir William Keith, governor of the Pennsylvania colony. As the two men talked,

Holmes told Keith about his runaway brother-in-law, and showed him Franklin's letter. Franklin's writing exercises paid off. Governor Keith was very impressed by the letter's wit and clarity, and he promised to do whatever he could to help this unknown young man who wrote so well.

One day not long afterward, as Franklin and Keimer were at work in the shop, two finely dressed gentlemen appeared at the door. At once Keimer recognized one of them as Governor Keith and grew giddy with excitement. Keimer must have thought the esteemed visitor had come

Governor Keith visiting Keimer's print shop.

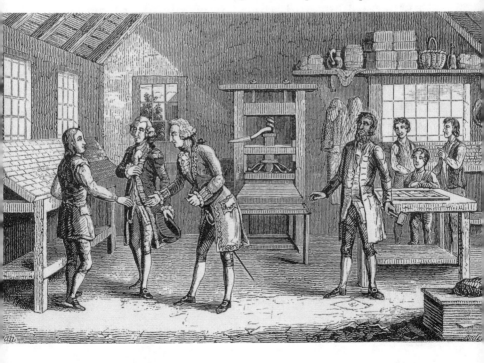

to see him, perhaps to discuss some official documents that needed printing. Instead, the governor asked only after his new assistant. He introduced himself to Franklin, showered him with compliments, and invited him to a nearby tavern.

Franklin had no idea how Keith had heard of him. But he responded warmly to the governor's attention and left his work to set out for the tavern. In his autobiography, he wrote, "I was not a little surpriz'd, and Keimer star'd like a Pig poison'd."

Over the finest Madeira wine in town, the governor told Franklin that he should open his own printing business. Good printers were scarce in Philadelphia, and there was plenty of work. Franklin seemed a bright, determined young man with a promising future. If he would set up a shop, Keith could make him the official printer for the colonies of Pennsylvania and Delaware. He could not lend him any money to get started, but surely Franklin could borrow the necessary capital from his father.

At eighteen, barely finished with his apprenticeship, Franklin must have been dazzled. His father could not possibly refuse him a loan, when he heard that the governor himself was eager to help. He only needed to go and ask in person.

Late in April 1724, seven months after his furtive departure, Franklin made a triumphant journey home to Boston.

5
Benjamin Franklin, Printer

Franklin's parents were thrilled to see him again, happy and healthy and full of plans. He looked taller than they remembered, and he walked with a new confidence. But after the excitement wore off, things did not go smoothly. Nothing Franklin said would persuade his father to finance his printing venture. Josiah Franklin felt that the governor had not thought out his offer very carefully. After all, Franklin was still only a boy, too young to run his own business.

When Franklin visited his brother James, he found that their past differences were neither forgiven nor forgotten. James resented his younger brother, who had fled his responsibilities in Boston. Now here was Ben again, swaggering back, his pockets jingling with silver coins. Many years would pass before James and Benjamin were finally at peace with one another.

Before he left for Philadelphia again, Franklin paid a visit to his brother's old enemy, Cotton Mather. Mather received him cordially, and they had a long conversation about books. As Franklin rose to go, Mather warned him that he was approaching a low doorway. Franklin did not duck soon enough, and bumped his head. "You are young, and have the world before you," Mather told him. "Stoop as you go through it, and you will miss many hard bumps."

Back in Philadelphia, Franklin still found Governor Keith full of encouragement. The governor urged him to go to London and buy the type, paper, and press he needed to open a shop. Keith promised to give him letters that would allow him to buy everything on credit. He could pay back the loans when he began to earn money. With a friend, James Ralph, Franklin prepared for the voyage to England.

In the weeks before his departure, Franklin and Deborah Read talked seriously of getting married. But Deborah's mother urged them to wait. When Franklin left, no promises had been made.

The governor told Franklin that the letters of credit would be waiting when he boarded his ship. But when the ship set sail, the letters were nowhere to be found. The captain told Franklin that he had a bag full of important papers in his cabin. The governor's letters were probably there. He would hand them over as soon as they reached London.

When the ship finally docked after weeks at sea, Franklin went to the captain again. But when the bag was opened, it contained no letters addressed to Benjamin Franklin. After all the plans and promises, Governor Keith had failed to keep his word. It must have been a crushing disappointment. But by the time he wrote his autobiography, Franklin recalled the governor with gentle understanding. "He wish'd to please every body," he wrote, "and having little to give, he gave Expectations."

Franklin arrived in London in December of 1724. He found himself in the biggest and busiest city in Europe. The air was often thick with smog from the constant burning of coal fires. Hawkers thronged the streets, peddling everything from shoes to strawberries. Franklin was astonished by the number of shops that sold books. He must have felt like a starving man walking into a banquet hall.

Once more Franklin was adrift in an unknown city, and once more he found work in a print shop. James Ralph was less successful in finding a job, and borrowed heavily from Franklin. Like most of the young men Franklin met in London, Ralph enjoyed drinking in the local pubs. Franklin was never a heavy drinker. In fact, his friends nick-

Franklin's residence in London.

named him "the Water American" because he preferred water to beer.

Ralph soon took a fancy to a pretty young hat-maker, and forgot his wife and baby daughter in Philadelphia. Franklin, too, seemed to put aside his attachments back home. During his stay in London, he sent only one letter to Deborah Read. In it he told her he might remain permanently in England.

Yet, after working for eighteen months in London, Franklin decided to return to America. The voyage home was uneventful, and he had plenty of time to think and to write. He recorded many of his observations in a daily journal. Always intrigued by the natural world, he wrote about the dolphins which cavorted around the ship. He described crabs, flying fish, and a solar eclipse.

During this journey, Franklin launched a program of self-improvement that he followed, with occasional lapses, for the rest of his life. "I conceiv'd the bold and arduous Project of arriving at moral Perfection," he explained in his autobiography. "I wish'd to live without committing any Fault at any time."

To achieve this extraordinary goal, he decided to acquire a series of human virtues systematically, one by one. His list of virtues reads, in part:

> Temperance — Eat not to Dullness. Drink not to Elevation.
>
> Silence — Speak not but what may benefit others or yourself. Avoid trifling Conversation.
>
> Order — Let all your Things have their Places; let each Part of your Business have its Time.
>
> Frugality — Make no Expense but to do good to others or yourself; i.e., Waste nothing.

Cleanliness — Tolerate no Uncleanli-
ness in Body, Clothes, or Habitation.

The list also included resolution, industry, sin-
cerity, justice, moderation, tranquility, and
chastity.

Some months later, when he showed his list to
his friends in Philadelphia, they suggested that
he tackle one more virtue: humility. They seemed
to agree with Cotton Mather that it might be wise
for Franklin to stoop a bit as he went through the
world. Franklin added humility to his list. He
admitted that he found it the hardest of all of the
virtues to achieve. No sooner did he make progress, than he would catch himself feeling proud
of his accomplishment.

Many changes greeted Franklin when he arrived in Philadelphia in 1726. One of his closest
friends, Joseph Watson, had died. Another friend,
Charles Osborne, had moved to the West Indies.
William Keith had been removed from his office
as governor of Pennsylvania. And Deborah Read,
after receiving Franklin's letter from England,
had married someone else. Her husband, a potter
named Rogers, had mistreated her and eventually, like Osborne, left for the West Indies. Now
she did not know if he was alive or dead.

For a while Franklin put aside his dreams of
starting his own business, and went back to work
with Samuel Keimer. The two got along no better
than before. Keimer had an explosive temper,

and Franklin could cling stubbornly to his own opinions. Once, after an argument, Franklin stormed off, leaving all his belongings behind. But a few days later, Keimer asked him to return. He had been commissioned to print paper money for the New Jersey colony, and he knew Franklin could handle the job better than anyone else. The quarrel forgotten, Franklin went back to work.

But after a year, Franklin left Keimer forever. With another printer, Hugh Meredith, he opened a shop of his own. Meredith's father donated money to help the two get started. Like James Ralph, Meredith had a drinking problem. His father hoped that Franklin would be a good influence in Hugh's life.

Franklin and Meredith opened their shop in 1728 — the third printing establishment in Philadelphia. Keimer was outraged, and tried to undercut their business. In 1728 he launched a newspaper, the *Pennsylvania Gazette*. Franklin and Meredith did not have the funds to compete by starting a paper of their own. Instead, they began publishing a column called "The Busy-Body" in Andrew Bradford's paper.

"The Busy-Body" was a series of humorous pieces about local people and events that were probably well-known to most of the paper's readers. Like the Silence Dogood letters in the *New England Courant*, many of these pieces appeared as letters by fictitious citizens. In one, a shopkeeper named "Patience" complained about a customer who let her children run wild through her store. "Sometimes they pull the books off my low shelves down to the ground, and perhaps where one of them has just been making water. [The mother] takes up the stuff and cries: 'Eh, thou little wicked mischievous rogue! But, however, it has done no great damage; 'tis only wet a little'; and so puts it up upon the shelf again."

"The Busy-Body" was immensely popular. In the meantime, Keimer fell deeper and deeper into debt. At last, in 1729, he sold his business to Franklin and Meredith, and emigrated to the Caribbean island of Barbados.

Not even Franklin's sober influence could keep Hugh Meredith out of the taverns and gaming houses. Eventually Meredith announced that he was simply not cut out to be a printer. He had heard that land was cheap in North Carolina, and decided to go and try his hand at farming. Franklin bought out his share of their joint venture. As a farewell gift he gave him a saddle for his long ride. Meredith set off, leaving Franklin sole owner of the business.

Franklin was not only a skilled printer, but a shrewd businessman as well. Like a modern politician, he cultivated a good public image. To show the people of Philadelphia that he was a hard worker, he personally pushed loads of paper through the streets in a wheelbarrow.

Most of the material Franklin printed was religious in nature — hymnals and sermons. But his special pride was the *Pennsylvania Gazette*. He introduced his first issue with a preface that stated, "To publish a good newspaper is not so easy an undertaking as many people imagine it to be. The author of a gazette . . . ought to be qualified with an extensive acquaintance with languages, a great easiness and command of writing. . . . He should be able to speak of war both by land and sea; be well acquainted with geography, with the history of the time, with the several interests of princes and states, the secrets of courts, and the manners and customs of all nations. Men thus accomplished are very rare in this remote part of the world."

In colonial Philadelphia, an almanac was often the only book a family possessed. These early almanacs included information about the stars and the phases of the moon, hints on farming and home management, and a monthly calendar. In 1732, Benjamin Franklin began to publish an almanac of his own. In addition to the usual information, it was stocked with the wise sayings, or proverbs, of its "author," whom Franklin called Richard Saunders. The proverbs usually began with the phrase "Poor Richard says," and thus the almanac is remembered as *Poor Richard's Almanac.*

A new edition of *Poor Richard's Almanac* appeared every year between 1732 and 1757. Many of its proverbs celebrated industry and frugality:

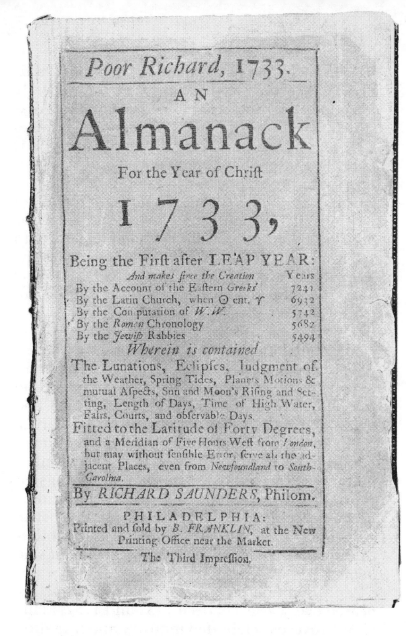

Poor Richard, 1733.

AN

Almanack

For the Year of Christ

1733,

Being the First after LEAP YEAR:

And makes since the Creation Years
By the Account of the Eastern Greeks 7241
By the Latin Church, when ☉ ent. ♈ 6932
By the Computation of *W.W.* 5742
By the *Roman* Chronology 5682
By the *Jewish* Rabbies 5494

Wherein is contained

The Lunations, Eclipses, Judgment of the Weather, Spring Tides, Planets Motions & mutual Aspects, Sun and Moon's Rising and Setting, Length of Days, Time of High Water, Fairs, Courts, and observable Days.

Fitted to the Latitude of Forty Degrees, and a Meridian of Five Hours West from *London*, but may without sensible Error, serve all the adjacent Places, even from *Newfoundland* to *South-Carolina.*

By *RICHARD SAUNDERS*, Philom.

PHILADELPHIA:
Printed and sold by *B. FRANKLIN*, at the New Printing-Office near the Market.

The Third Impression.

The title page of the 1733 edition of Franklin's Poor Richard's Almanac.

"Early to bed and early to rise/ Makes a man healthy, wealthy and wise," or "Then plow deep while sluggards sleep,/ And you shall have corn to sell and keep." The writer Mark Twain once claimed that the lives of a million schoolboys had been made miserable by Franklin's nagging advice.

But not all Poor Richard's comments were meant to be elevating. The 1733 almanac included some verses by Richard Saunders on the idleness of women. In 1734 Richard's wife Bridget responded with verses of her own, on the worthlessness of men. Their quarrel kept up through the next several editions. Then, in 1738, Bridget went through the entire almanac while her husband was away, scratching out his comments and adding her own. "Cannot I have a little fault or two but all the country must see it in print?" she demanded in her preface. She improved the weather Richard had forecast "for the goodwomen to dry their clothes in."

Poor Richard's Almanac became immensely popular, selling 10,000 copies a year. In 1757, for the twenty-fifth and final edition, Franklin collected many of his favorite proverbs into a long essay called "The Way to Wealth." Richard Saunders presented this essay as a speech he heard delivered at an auction by an old man, Father Abraham. Father Abraham's speech is full of wisdom about working hard and saving money: "Industry pays debts, while despair increases them";

Two illustrated versions of the proverbs from
Poor Richard's Almanac.

"There are no gains without pains"; "He that lives on hope will die fasting"; "Not to oversee workmen is to leave them your purse open."

"The Way to Wealth" has been reprinted countless times, and its sayings are woven into the American character. Today Father Abraham's proverbs often come to mind when we think of Benjamin Franklin. But to the people of colonial Philadelphia, Franklin was also Richard Saunders, with his earthy wit, quarreling year after year with his wife.

6
Private Life and Public Improvements

As his printing business expanded, Franklin was busy rekindling his friendship with Deborah Read. She had learned that Rogers, her husband, may already have been married to someone else at the time he married her. Thus, she may never have been his legal wife at all. She had not heard from him in years and suspected that he was dead.

Although the legality of their union was uncertain, Benjamin Franklin and Deborah Read were married on September 1, 1730. Deborah was a simple, quiet woman, and lacked Franklin's intellectual curiosity. But through all the years and changes that lay ahead, she remained loyal and patient. "We throve together," Franklin wrote in his autobiography, "and have ever mutually endeavor'd to make each other happy."

Deborah's loyalty and patience faced a hard test in the first months of her marriage, when Franklin asked her to help raise his illegitimate son, William. The identity of William's mother remains a mystery to this day. Whoever she was, she left her baby entirely in Franklin's care.

William grew up as a full member of the Franklin household. Deborah and Benjamin had two other children — Francis Folger, born in 1732, and Sarah, who arrived in 1743.

Benjamin Franklin wrote little about his family life. A few details can be gathered from notices which he placed in the *Gazette*. In 1734, when William was only four and Francis two, Franklin advertised for "a servant . . . that is a scholar and can teach children reading, writing and arithmetic." Eight years later, the *Gazette* promised free rides to any boy who might find and return William's lost mare.

In 1733, Franklin revisited family and friends in New England. He had not seen his brother James in ten years, and now found him frail and ill. In the event of his death, James asked Benjamin to take care of his son and teach him the printing trade. When James died two years later, his twelve-year-old son came to live in Philadelphia. By providing for this nephew, Franklin felt that he had finally paid back the old debt of the broken apprenticeship.

In 1736, four-year-old Francis Fogler died of smallpox. Rumors buzzed through Philadelphia that the boy had died after being inoculated. Though he had opposed inoculation back in Boston, Franklin had come to recognize its value in controlling the disease. Shortly after his son's death, he put an end to the rumors with a brief article in the *Gazette*. He explained that he had planned to have Francis inoculated, but had not done so in time to save his life.

Franklin may never have fully reconciled himself to the loss of his younger son. When he was well into middle age he wrote to his sister Jane Mecom, "Of my son Franky, now dead thirty-six Years, whom I have seldom since seen equal'd in every thing, and whom to this Day I cannot think of without a Sigh."

Franklin spent his days in his print shop, running off newspapers and advertisements. He also found time, with the help of Deborah and her mother, to operate a general store in the front room of his home. The shelves overflowed with a jumble of items: soap, sealing wax, quill pens, spectacles, compasses, maps, and fishnets. There were imported foods: Rhode Island cheeses, dried cod from Massachusetts, Spanish wine, and tea and spices from China. At one counter, customers could buy salves, poultices, and other home remedies concocted by Deborah's mother. In fact, the Franklins were willing to sell almost anything — including African slaves. One advertisement

An advertisement for a slave auction.

posted outside the shop read: "a likely Negro wench about fifteen years old, has had the small-pox, been in the country above a year and talks English. Inquire of the printer hereof."

One corner of the shop was set aside as the local post office. Bags of mail flowed in and out, from New England, the Carolinas, Europe, and the West Indies. Franklin had the chance to read newspapers from all over the English-speaking world.

In those early years of the shop and the printing business, the family had little money to spare for frills. But one morning, Franklin was amazed to see a fine china bowl and silver spoon on the table before him. His wife explained that she had bought them, because he deserved the same luxuries his neighbors enjoyed.

Franklin was a tireless worker. But his mind needed challenges that business alone could not provide. He wanted to discuss books and ideas with other people who shared his passion for learning. In 1727, while he was still working for Samuel Keimer, he founded a weekly discussion group called the Junto. Most of its members were tradesmen. Hugh Meredith, Stephen Potts, and George Webb were all printers. Joseph Breintnal was a copier of deeds, Nicholas Scull and William Parsons were surveyors. William Maugridge was a mechanic, and William Coleman was a merchant's clerk. Only Robert Grace was "a young gentleman of some fortune."

Like Franklin, the other members of the Junto all possessed many interests and talents. Gathering at a Philadelphia tavern on Friday nights, they debated the nature of happiness, the meaning of wisdom, and such perplexing questions as why the outside of a glass of cold water is beaded with moisture on a summer day.

The Junto met regularly for the next thirty years, and its members became some of Philadelphia's leading citizens. Scull and Parsons became surveyor generals, responsible for the division and development of much of the land in southeastern Pennsylvania. Coleman went on to become a judge. Robert Grace, a noted manufacturer, eventually promoted the new heating stove Franklin invented.

The group launched many projects for the city's improvement. One of these was a lending library, the first in the thirteen colonies. The library

Franklin opened the first lending library in colonial America.

opened in Pewter Platter Alley in 1731. It was not open to the general public, but limited to members who paid a "subscription," or fee. Paying subscribers could browse or borrow on Saturdays between 12 and 4, or on Wednesdays from 2 to 3 in the afternoon.

The members of the Junto aided one another in many ways. They lent each other money and helped each other obtain work and advancement. When Franklin suggested that Philadelphians needed protection from fires, the Junto gave him

A volunteer fire department puts out a fire in early America.

its full support. In 1736, Franklin established Philadelphia's first volunteer fire department. He also tried to improve the street patrol, or watch — the forerunner of today's police department. The watch was corrupt and inefficient, and change came reluctantly. Franklin concluded that it was far easier to create a brand-new system than to improve one that was already established.

Even after the success of the Junto, Franklin was still hungry for contact with other intellectuals. Surely, throughout the colonies, there must be scientists and philosophers, mathematicians and inventors working in isolation. Perhaps they could correspond with one another and could even meet from time to time to share their ideas and discoveries. To foster communication among the learned men of the colonies, Franklin founded the American Philosophical Society.

The American Philosophical Society met once a year at its headquarters in Philadelphia. At these meetings, members read papers describing their research and discoveries. Between meetings, they kept in contact with one another by visiting and writing letters.

Still based in Philadelphia, the American Philosophical Society survives to this day. Among its members have been some two hundred winners of the prestigious Nobel prize. These Nobel laureates include the chemist Linus Pauling, geneticist Barbara McClintock, economist Paul

Samuelson, physicist Frank Yang, and Francis Crick and James P. Watson, who helped to unravel the structure of the DNA molecule. By creating a forum where such great minds could come together, Franklin left the world an enduring legacy.

7
The Fire from the Sky

From time to time, Franklin may have seen magicians perform in taverns or on the public square. Sometimes these tricksters used a mysterious force that they called "electrical fire." The electrical fire could make a spark leap from the end of a boy's nose, or cause a girl's hair to stand on end.

On a trip to Boston in 1743, Franklin met a Scottish scientist, Dr. Archibald Spencer, who was studying the electrical fire on a more serious level. Franklin was fascinated. Back in Philadelphia, he purchased metal plates, glass tubes, and wires, and plunged into a series of experiments.

Franklin was now a prosperous businessman of forty. In a portrait done at this time, perhaps by the noted painter Robert Feke, he has a determined chin and a bold, fierce gaze. It is the face of a hard-working, self-made man. Franklin had worked tirelessly to build his printing business, always saving money for the future. But now that future had arrived. He had discovered a new purpose in life, and he could afford to set everything else aside. "I never was before engaged in any study that so totally engrossed my attention and my time," he wrote to the English botanist Peter Collinson, ". . . and, what with making experiments when I can be alone, and repeating them to my friends and acquaintances . . . I have during some months past had little leisure for anything else."

In 1748 Franklin left the printing business altogether, dedicating himself wholly to science. People paraded through his house — fellow scientists eager to help with his experiments, and passersby curious to see his electrical marvels. With an assortment of everyday household items — a salt shaker, a pump handle, the gold leaf from the binding of a book — he constructed machines that would hold or give off electrical energy.

Before Franklin began his work, scientists believed that there were two types of electricity. "Vitreous" electricity was produced by rubbing glass with silk. The "resinous" form was produced on resin rubbed with wool. Franklin was the first to recognize that electricity was, as he

A painting of Benjamin Franklin by Charles W. Peale.

called it, "a single fluid." He renamed the vitreous and resinous forms "positive" and "negative." To this day, we speak of positive and negative charges when discussing electricity.

In 1749 Franklin and his colleages put together a device which they called an electrical battery — the enormous, clumsy ancestor of the batteries that fuel our flashlights and tape players today. It consisted of eleven vertical panes of glass, placed two inches apart and suspended from thick silk cords. Between panes with positive and negative charges, electricity could be stored for further use.

Many people asked what possible use could be made of Franklin's electrical fire. He himself once suggested that, if nothing else, the wonders of electricity could benefit humanity by making vain men humble.

Franklin could not have imagined that by the twentieth century electricity would provide light and entertainment, would toast bread and keep milk cold, clean carpets, saw lumber, and wash clothes. But he clearly suspected that it could be a valuable source of power. Writing humorously to Peter Collinson, he described a picnic to be held on the banks of the Schuylkill River. "A turkey is to be killed for our dinner by the electrical shock, and roasted by the electrical jack, before a fire kindled by the electrified bottle; when the healths of all the famous electricians in England, Holland, France, and Germany are to be drunk in electrified bumpers, under the discharge of guns from the electrical battery."

Franklin did, in fact, try to kill a turkey by electrocution. Unfortunately, his experiment misfired, and he received a powerful shock himself. Always the scientist, Franklin described the sensation in detail. "I then felt . . . a universal blow throughout my whole body from head to foot, which seemed within as well as without; after which the first thing I took notice of was a violent quick shaking of my body, which gradually remitted, my sense as gradually returning. . . . That part of my hand and fingers which held the chain was left white, as though the blood had been driven out, . . . and I had a numbness in my arms and in the back of my neck which continued till the next morning but wore off." With his typical humor he added that the goose, not the turkey, was nearly cooked.

Franklin suspected that lightning was identical to the electrical fire he could capture between his glass panes. Nearly everyone has heard the story of the experiment with a kite that finally proved his theory. Yet Franklin himself never wrote about the kite experiment. The story was written down by a British scientist, Joseph Priestley, who apparently heard it from Franklin several years after it occurred. For this reason, some of the details remain vague. According to Priestley, Franklin made a kite from a silk handkerchief, and fastened a key to the end of the string. He

Ben Franklin's famous kite and key experiment.

invited his son William to help him fly the kite as a thunderstorm approached. (By tradition, artists have depicted William as a boy of about twelve, but he was actually twenty-one at the time.) Together they set the kite aloft over an open field and waited for results. For a while nothing happened. They were about to give up when Franklin noticed that some threads had come unraveled near the top of the string, and were now standing on end. Eagerly he touched the key and felt a definite shock. Lightning and electricity were one and the same.

In the 1753 edition of *Poor Richard's Almanac* Franklin put his new knowledge about lightning to practical use. To protect their houses and barns from lightning, he advised his readers to provide a small iron rod . . . of such a length that, one end being three or four feet in the moist ground, the other may be six or eight feet above the highest part of the building. To the upper end of the rod fasten about a foot of brass wire the size of a common knitting-needle, sharpened to a fine point. . . . A house thus furnished will not be damaged by lightning, it being attracted to the point and passing through the metal into the ground without hurting anything."

Franklin's lightning rods soon sprouted from houses, sheds, and churches throughout the colonies. But some people were suspicious of the strange new gadgets. When a mild earthquake shook the city of Boston, a newspaper article claimed that all the electricity pouring into the ground from Franklin's rods had brought on the tremor.

Franklin wrote regularly about his experiments to scientists in England, France, and Germany. He described much of his work in a pamphlet called "Experiments and Observations on Electricity, Made at Philadelphia in America." The pamphlet was translated into French, and French scientists carried out some of Franklin's experiments for their king.

The first publication of Franklin's experiments on electricity.

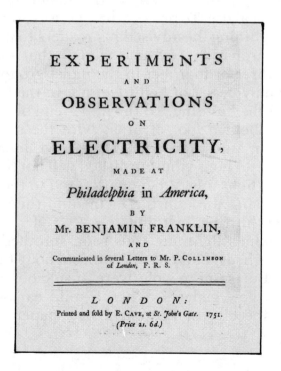

Meanwhile, back in Philadelphia, Franklin went on making electrical devices. He erected a rod on the roof of his house, passing it through the ceiling above the staircase. At the lower end of the rod, opposite the bedroom door, two bells hung from a wire with a brass ball swinging between them. The ball would strike and ring the bells whenever an electrical storm was brewing.

One night Franklin and his wife were awakened by loud crashing sounds. Franklin rushed onto the landing. Later he described the scene: "The brass ball, instead of vibrating as usual between the bells, was repelled and kept at a distance from both; while the fire passed, sometimes in a continued, dense, white stream, . . . whereby the whole staircase was inlighted as with sunshine, so that one might see to pick up a pin."

We can only try to imagine what Deborah Read must have thought of the commotion. Perhaps by that time she was used to the surprises and uncertainties of life with Benjamin Franklin. For years she contented herself with her husband's electrical experiments and with the people who tramped through her house to watch them. But what lay ahead may have been even more difficult for her. As time passed, she had to deal more and more with Franklin's long absences. The ambitious young printer she had married turned into a foreign diplomat and even ventured into a military campaign against the Indians.

8
General Benjamin Franklin

While Franklin was busy experimenting with electricity, he remained passionately committed to public affairs. He was a tireless worker and, although he was never a strong public speaker, he could express his ideas in writing with stunning clarity. Perhaps most important of all, Franklin was gifted in the art of winning people's confidence and respect. He made friends wherever he went. As the colonial leaders grew to trust him and to value his opinions, Franklin's influence spread even wider. Gradually it reached beyond Philadelphia to all of Pennsylvania, beyond Pennsylvania to the other colonies, and finally to England and France.

In his autobiography, Franklin offered a bit of

advice to politicians: "Never ask, never refuse, and never resign." Since 1736, he had been clerk of the Pennsylvania Assembly. In 1751 he was elected to serve as one of the assembly's burgesses, or representatives. In the same year he was chosen to act as an alderman in Philadelphia.

Despite his public acclaim, Franklin could not forget that he came from humble beginnings. When he wrote to his mother about his latest office, she replied, "I am glad to hear that you are so respected in your town for them to choose you alderman, although I don't know what it means, nor what the better you will be of it besides the honor of it."

The library and the fire department were not Franklin's only contributions to Philadelphia. In 1749 he helped to establish the Philadelphia Academy, a school for boys between the ages of eight and sixteen. Franklin wrote that the boys should be taught "everything that is useful and everything that is ornamental," including how to swim. The academy eventually became the University of Pennsylvania.

Franklin also promoted the founding of Philadelphia's first hospital. According to Franklin's inscription on the cornerstone, the hospital was created "for the relief of the sick and miserable." In addition to those suffering a variety of physical maladies, "the sick and miserable" included the mentally ill, who often wandered through the streets, desperate and lost.

This statue on the campus of the University of Pennsylvania shows Franklin as he arrived, penniless, in Philadelphia at the age of 17.

Ever since the colonies were founded, the British government had seen them as a convenient place to send men and women convicted of crimes. The British insisted that this practice was for the "improvement and well peopling" of the colonies. Franklin's first task as a member of the Assembly was to draft a bill of protest. But his finest writing on the matter appeared in the *Pennsylvania Gazette*. With his usual wit, he suggested that, in return for Britain's generous donation of convicts, the colonies should send rattlesnakes to England. "There I would propose to have them carefully distributed to St. James's Park, in the Spring Gardens and other places of pleasure about London; in the gardens of all the nobility and gentry throughout the nation; but particularly in the gardens of the prime ministers, the lords of trade, and members of Parliament, for to them we are most particularly obliged."

Since his early days as a printer, when bags of mail filled one corner of his shop, Franklin had been concerned with the improvement of postal service in the colonies. The colonies functioned as completely separate entities. Each one even had its own form of money. If the colonies were linked more tightly together, Franklin realized, mail could move more efficiently between them. Together the colonies could even tackle such problems as the export of convicts from Britain. In 1754 Franklin published what is probably America's first political cartoon. It was the draw-

Probably America's first political cartoon, this depicts the colonies as a snake cut into pieces.

ing of a snake cut into eight pieces. The pieces were labeled New England, New York, New Jersey, Pennsylvania, Maryland, Virginia, North Carolina, and South Carolina. The caption read: "Join, or die."

That same year Franklin attended a convention in Albany, New York, to work out a peace treaty with the Iroquois Indians. Representatives from several of the colonies were present. Franklin took the opportunity to suggest a plan for greater colonial unity. But no one else seemed interested.

In contrast with the scattered British colonies, the Iroquois had a strong confederation of six Indian nations. "It would be a strange thing if six nations of [Native Americans] should be capable of forming a scheme for such a union," Franklin wrote, ". . . and yet that a like union should be impracticable for ten or a dozen English colonies, to whom it is more necessary and must be more advantageous."

Although Franklin respected the achievements of the Iroquois, he harbored deep prejudices against other ethnic groups. He was alarmed by the growing numbers of German settlers in Pennsylvania and wrote, "Why should the Palatine boors be suffered to swarm into our settlement and, by herding together, establish their language and manners to the exclusion of ours?" He opposed slavery, but not from horror at the capture and sale of fellow human beings. "Why increase the sons of Africa by planting them in America," he demanded, "where we have so fair an opportunity, by excluding all blacks and tawnys, of increasing the lovely red and white?" On second thought, however, he may have realized that he was being narrow-minded, for he added, "But perhaps I am partial to the complexion of my country, for such kind of partiality is natural to mankind."

For decades, the French and English had struggled for control of the American frontier. In 1754 the conflict erupted into the French and Indian War. The French encouraged their Indian allies to attack remote settlements in Pennsylvania. One night a Shawnee band swept down on the unsuspecting German village of Gnadenhutten, about seventy-five miles from Philadelphia. The Indians set cabins ablaze and killed men, women, and children.

Founded by peace-loving Quakers, Pennsylvania had never developed a strong militia. But now even the Quakers in the Assembly admitted that the colony needed to defend itself. Hastily, an expedition set off for the troubled frontier. Among its leaders was Assemblyman Benjamin Franklin, with his son William as his aide.

In his youth Franklin was sturdy and muscular. But by now some of his muscles had gone to flesh. He was a stout gentleman of fifty, whose life had been devoted to books, business, and scientific investigation. Yet he adjusted at once to the rigors of a military campaign. For two months he traveled on horseback from one settlement to another, sleeping in tents and eating sparse, poorly cooked meals. Although he saw no actual combat, he went on scouting expeditions, evaluated military defenses, and supervised the construction of a log stockade.

One day a supply wagon arrived with a special treat — a meal of veal and beef sent by Franklin's wife. "Your citizens that have their dinners hot know nothing of good eating," he wrote to her in thanks. "We find it in much greater perfection when the kitchen is fourscore miles from the dining-room."

When Franklin finally returned home, the governor appointed him colonel in the Philadelphia militia. But the German settlers along the frontier always called him General Benjamin Franklin.

9
An Agent to England

Since its founding in 1682, the Pennsylvania colony had been ruled by the Penn family. Unfortunately, William Penn's sons and grandsons did not share his commitment to the colony's welfare. They controlled it from faraway England, seldom crossing the Atlantic to visit their property. Though they owned vast estates, they paid no land taxes for the colony's support.

When Benjamin Franklin became a colonel in the Pennsylvania militia, the Penns were dismayed. They feared that he was becoming too powerful, and that some day he might work to overthrow them. "I am not much concerned by that," Franklin wrote humorously to Peter Collinson, "because if I have offended them by acting right, I can, whenever I please, reverse their displeasure by acting wrong."

In 1757, the Pennsylvania Assembly appointed Franklin to serve as its agent in London. He was to present a number of grievances to the Penns, including the demand that they pay taxes on their landholdings.

Franklin and his son William reached London in July 1757. With their two servants (one of whom, a slave named King, ran away after a year) they rented four rooms in a house on Craven Street. In one room, Franklin set up his scientific laboratory. Another room was used for entertaining visitors.

Visitors flocked to the house on Craven Street. For years Franklin had corresponded with some of London's most learned men. Now, to his great delight, he could meet them in person. The botanist Peter Collinson dropped by frequently. So did Joseph Priestley, the renowned chemist, and the printer and publisher William Strahan. Dr. John Fothergill came to share his latest medical theories. "I never saw a man who was, in every respect, so perfectly agreeable to me," Strahan wrote. "Some are amiable in one view, some in another; he in all."

The Penn family, however, did not share Strahan's enthusiasm. "He is a dangerous man," wrote John Penn, governor of Pennsylvania, "and I should be very glad if he inhabited another country, as I believe him of a very uneasy spirit."

For his part, Franklin had no fondness for any of the Penns. One acquaintance wrote that his face sometimes turned "white as the driven snow with the extremes of wrath" when he spoke to them. As soon as he arrived in London, he presented the Penns with the colonists' grievances. But five years passed before they finally agreed to pay taxes on their land in America.

Naturally, Franklin did not sit idle while he waited for the Penns to act. He worked on electrical experiments. He discussed philosophy with friends in London coffeehouses. He tracked down long-lost relatives. As he had done in Boston and Philadelphia, he wrote letters to newspaper editors, signed with fictitious names.

He also developed an interest in music, and invented an instrument which he called the glass harmonica. It consisted of thirty-seven hemispheres of glass, arranged according to size. The glasses turned when the player pressed a pedal. By touching the moving glass pieces with moistened fingers, the player produced a variety of notes. For about thirty years the glass harmonica was widely played, inspiring compositions by Mozart and Beethoven.

Franklin was immensely popular with the ladies of London, as well as with the gentlemen. Soon after his arrival, William Strahan wrote playfully to Deborah, urging her to join her husband lest he be led astray by one of his many admirers. Deborah, however, insisted that she

Franklin playing the glass harmonica, an instrument he invented.

could never bring herself to make the treacherous voyage across the Atlantic. She was still as quiet and retiring as she had been when she married. Perhaps she felt overwhelmed by her husband's important friends and unable to enter his social circle. Whatever her reason, she stayed steadfastly at home in Philadelphia.

If Deborah had had a jealous nature, marriage to Franklin would have been agony. He reveled in the company of women, and women lavished attention upon him. Two years before he set out for England, he met a young Rhode Island woman, Catherine Ray, who sent him a series of yearning love letters. Apparently Franklin flirted with her in the beginning. But his surviving letters indicate that he quickly toned down the relationship. Friendship was fine, but he would be faithful to his wife. "Mrs. Franklin was very proud that a young lady should have so much regard for her old husband," he wrote to Catherine. "[She] talks of bequeathing me to you as a legacy; but I . . . hope she will live these hundred years; for we are grown old together, and if she has any faults I am so used to 'em that I don't perceive 'em."

In London, Franklin found a special friend in Polly Stevenson, his landlady's twenty-one-year-old daughter. Polly was pretty and charming, but best of all, she had a keen mind and a lively interest in science. There may have been a flirtatious smile or two scattered through their discussions about plants and minerals. But once again, Franklin kept the relationship from becoming romantic. When Polly married, he remained close to her and to her husband, and acted as godfather to their children.

Throughout Franklin's stay in London, he and Deborah exchanged many long letters full of news. He sent her cases of presents — fine fabrics, china, wines, and cheese. One gift was a large barrel that he felt "looked like a fat jolly dame, clean and tidy, with a neat blue and white calico gown on, good-natured and lovely."

In 1758, William completed a degree in law. Soon after, father and son traveled to Scotland, where they made new friends and explored the wild countryside. In a letter to Deborah, Strahan commented that Franklin was "his son's friend, his brother, his intimate and easy companion."

Just before the Franklins returned to Philadelphia, William married Elizabeth Downes, a young British woman who had grown up in the West Indies. He was also appointed to serve as governor of the New Jersey colony, a surprise and a great honor for a man of only thirty-one.

Franklin remained in England until 1762. Despite the long separation from his family, those five years may have been the happiest of his entire life. Preparing for the voyage home he wrote to his Scottish friend, Lord Kames, "I am going from the old world to the new; and I fancy I feel like those who are leaving this world for the next:

grief at the parting; fear of the passage; hope of the future."

A few months after Franklin returned to Pennsylvania, a band of ruffians massacred a group of Indians near the town of Lancaster. The massacre was in retaliation for an earlier Indian raid against a white settlement. Tragically, the Indians who were killed had had nothing to do with the previous fighting.

Years before, Franklin had expressed his own prejudices in statements against Germans and Africans. But now, perhaps with the wisdom of age, he wrote an eloquent essay against racial discrimination. Referring to the massacre, he wrote, "The only crime of these poor wretches seems to have been that they had a reddish-brown skin and black hair; and some people of that sort, it seems, have murdered some of our relations. If it be right to kill men for such reason, then should any man with a freckled face and red hair kill a wife or child of mine, it would be right for me to revenge it by killing all the freckled red-haired men, women, and children I could afterwards anywhere meet with."

In 1763 the French surrendered, bringing the French and Indian War to a close at last. But the long conflict had emptied the British treasury. In London, Parliament thought of ways to raise fresh revenue. One way was to tax the colonies in America.

In 1765 Parliament passed the Stamp Act. The

colonists would have to purchase an official stamp whenever they obtained documents such as wills and property deeds. Stamps would also be required when they bought newspapers, stationery, and even playing cards.

British citizens living in England already paid a similar stamp tax. But they, at least, were represented by voting delegates in Parliament. The colonists had no representative to speak for them. From Massachusetts to New York, from New York to Pennsylvania, the angry words rang out: "Taxation without representation is tyranny!"

This colonial cartoon protested the Stamp Act.

The Pennsylvania Assembly appointed Franklin to go back to England and speak to Parliament. Perhaps he could bring about the repeal of the hated Stamp Act. Or, even better, he might persuade Parliament to grant the colonies a greater voice in their own government.

Franklin was nearly sixty, and he was beginning to feel his age. Recently he had suffered two serious falls. He knew that if he went to England again, he would be gone for a long time — perhaps for the rest of his life. Though he had been happy in London, he hated to leave his home and family once more. Vainly he tried to convince Deborah to go with him. But she refused, still claiming she was afraid to cross the stormy Atlantic. They parted in November 1764. Franklin never saw her again.

Only weeks before his departure, Franklin had lost his seat in the Assembly after a hard-fought election. But he was still enormously popular. When word reached Philadelphia that he had arrived safely in London, joyous church bells rangs until midnight. Franklin's old friends from the Junto sat up together most of the night, reminiscing about the past thirty years.

Despite Franklin's best efforts, however, Parliament voted to pass the Stamp Act. "We might as well have hindered the sun's setting," he wrote to his friends back home. "That we cannot do. But since 'tis done, let us make as good a night of it as we can. We may still light candles."

Philadelphia surged with ugly rumors. Franklin was really working for the British. He had helped to engineer the Stamp Act, and some of the profits would flow into his own pockets. This was worse than anything Pennsylvania had endured from the Penn family.

William Franklin left the governor's mansion in New Jersey and rushed to check on his mother and sister. Enemies had threatened to burn their house to the ground. Sarah left with her brother, but Deborah was determined to stay in Philadelphia. She firmly believed that she had more friends than enemies, and that no harm would come to her. One of her brothers and one of her husband's nephews moved into the house with her, bringing a supply of muskets and powder. But as Deborah predicted, the Franklin home was never attacked.

In London, Franklin continued to argue against the Stamp Act. One of the act's promoters asked him if there was any change, or amendment, which could possibly make it more acceptable to the Americans. Franklin replied that there was, a simple change of only one word. "It is in that clause where it is said that from and after the first day of November, one thousand seven hundred and sixty-five, there shall be paid, etc. The amendment I would propose is, for *one* read *two*, and then all the rest of the act may stand as it does."

Franklin was still deeply loyal to the mother

country. He wanted the American colonies to be part of a strong, invincible British empire. But he feared that the Stamp Act (which he called "the mother of all mischief") would destroy any hope for unity between the colonies and England. If British troops tried to enforce the Stamp Act, Franklin warned Parliament, "they will not find a rebellion; they may indeed make one."

Back in the colonies, protest continued. In Massachusetts, stamp distributors were burned in effigy. In Connecticut, the distributor was driven from his home, his life threatened. At last, early in 1766, Parliament repealed the Stamp Act.

This cartoon celebrating the demise of the Stamp Act depicts it being laid to rest in a miniature coffin.

From New England to the Carolinas, bells clamored in celebration. Coffeehouses in Philadelphia gave presents to every man on the ship that brought the good news. Any lingering doubts about Franklin's loyalty to the colonies were set aside. All over the city, men drank his health. Benjamin Franklin, ambassador, was the hero of the day.

10
The Reluctant
Revolutionary

Much as he loved London, Franklin was often homesick. After the repeal of the Stamp Act, he was eager to return to Philadelphia. But soon Parliament passed the Townshend Acts, which levied a new series of taxes upon the colonies. The Townshend Acts placed import duties on glass, paint, linen, tea, and a long list of other everyday items.

Once more the colonies buzzed with outrage, but Parliament held firm. Insults and threats flew back and forth across the Atlantic. Franklin had no choice but to remain in London. As the official agent of Pennsylvania (and later of Georgia and Massachusetts) it was his duty to negotiate.

Franklin was dismayed by the growing hostility between England and the colonies. He still hoped that the colonies would keep a close connection with the mother country. He was convinced that both would be stronger as a result. But Parliament's harsh, insensitive treatment was pushing the colonies farther and farther away. Franklin compared the British Empire to a fine, noble china vase, exquisitely made, but fragile if it were not handled with care.

If England would only show them more respect, Franklin believed the colonists would be happy to remain British subjects. But few mem-

This colonial cartoon depicts America as a horse, rearing up to throw off its master, England.

bers of Parliament listened to his views. As the years passed, Franklin grew ever more frustrated and disillusioned.

The British people knew hopelessly little about life in America. In his own unique way, Franklin set about to educate them. In one of his anonymous letters to a London paper, he teased his readers about their ignorance. American sheep, he claimed, were far superior to those in England, for "the very tails of the American sheep are so laden with wool that each has a car or wagon on four little wheels to support [it] and keep it from trailing on the ground." He insisted that great whales swam in the rivers of North America, and made spectacular leaps up the roaring Niagara Falls. We can only wonder how many readers took him seriously, and how many understood the joke.

Business on behalf of the colonies devoured Franklin's days. Yet he still found time for old friends and made many new ones as well. Twice a month he discussed politics and philosophy with a group of men who called themselves the Honest Whigs. He exchanged affectionate letters with Polly Stevenson. As always, Franklin's scientific curiosity was inexhaustible. He examined the teeth and bones of a mastodon that had recently been unearthed, and wrote about the effects of lead poisoning.

In 1771, Franklin began to write the story of his life. His autobiography was written as though it were a long letter to his son. Like *Poor Richard's Almanac*, it was full of useful instructions for getting ahead in the world. But also like the almanac, it was also spiced with humor and incidents from everyday life.

Franklin traveled widely in England, Scotland, and Ireland. He enjoyed meeting new people wherever he went, especially when they shared his scientific interests. But he never cared much for sightseeing, and avoided castles and monuments. "I confess," he wrote, "that if I could find in my travels a recipe for making parmesan cheese, it would give me more satisfaction than . . . any inscription from any old stone whatever."

One year followed another, and still Franklin could not go home. He missed his daugher Sarah's wedding. He was far away when her baby boy, Benjamin Franklin Bache, took his first steps. But Deborah was a faithful correspondent, filling her letters with rich detail. She also sent him gifts from Pennsylvania — cornmeal, buckwheat flour, dried apples and peaches. Once she even sent a tame gray squirrel, which he gave to the children of a friend.

Meanwhile, relations between England and the colonies grew more strained than ever. One grievance piled upon another. In 1770, British troops fired upon protesters in Boston, and five people were killed. The incident was remembered as the Boston Massacre. After the massacre, redcoated

Franklin's only daughter, Sarah Franklin Bache.

British soldiers patroled Boston's streets, their muskets ready to enforce the law. The other colonies rallied in support of Massachusetts. In one way or another, they had all experienced British arrogance, the high-handed dealings of the mother country.

A less imaginative writer might have published a list of the colonists' grievances, hoping to arouse British sympathy. But Franklin turned again to humor — although this time his laughter had a bitter note. In 1773 he wrote an essay called "Rules by Which a Great Empire May Be Reduced to a Small One." It was written as a letter of advice to a fictitious king, suggesting ways he might rid himself of unwanted colonies. His suggestions were remarkably similar to the things that Parliament and the king had been doing to their American colonies.

In the essay, Franklin urged the king to make sure that the colonists never had the same rights and privileges as people of the mother country. He should avoid appointing honest, hardworking men to serve as governors and judges, and be careful instead to select "broken gamesters" and "prodigals who have ruined their fortunes." He should tax the people relentlessly, and undermine their military defenses. If all of these things were done properly, Franklin concluded, the king could be free of his troublesome provinces forever.

Franklin had many dear friends in London. But his cleverness and his biting wit had also earned him many enemies. They waited eagerly for a chance to get him out of the way. They found their opportunity at last in the episode of the Hutchinson letters.

Franklin never told anyone who gave him the letters. Later he said only that he received them from "a gentleman of character and distinction." There were ten of them in all, letters that had been written by Massachusetts Governor Thomas

Hutchinson and Lieutenant Governor Andrew Oliver. Both men were Boston natives, but their sympathies lay with the British. Their homes had been vandalized during the uproar over the Stamp Act. They had never forgiven nor forgotten.

The letters showed all too plainly how Hutchinson and Oliver felt about the Massachusetts Assembly and the people of the colony. "Ignorant though they be," Hutchinson wrote, "yet the heads of Boston passed a number of weak but very criminal resolutions." Oliver contended that it was absurd for a colony to expect the same privileges that the parent nation enjoyed.

After studying the letters carefully, Franklin decided to send them to Thomas Cushing, a friend who lived in Boston. He instructed Cushing to show them to a select group of Massachusetts patriots. But this request for secrecy was ignored. Soon copies circulated throughout Boston. Passages appeared in Massachusetts newspapers. The assembly sent a petition to London, demanding that Hutchinson and Oliver be removed from office.

The petition dragged the story into the glaring light. Franklin accepted full responsibility for sending the letters to Boston. But his enemies in Parliament and at court were still not satisfied. They wanted to humiliate the upstart American, and to be rid of him once and for all.

On January 29, 1774, Franklin was called to a

hearing before the Privy Council. The Privy Council was a group of noblemen with great power in colonial affairs. It included some of the most august men in England — the Archbishop of Canterbury, the Bishop of London, and a formidable array of dukes and earls. Only one of the councilors was a staunch Franklin supporter.

Representing Governor Hutchinson was a young lawyer named Alexander Wedderburn. Wedderburn was famous for his skill in attacking his opponents and ripping them to pieces.

Wedderburn delivered a long, impassioned speech, full of venom against Franklin. He accused Franklin of stealing the letters. He declared that Franklin had made them public in order to spread further discontent in the colonies. "I hope, my lords, you will mark and brand this man, for the honor of this country, of Europe, and of mankind," he stated. "He has forfeited all the respect of societies and of men."

Dressed in a suit of blue Manchester velvet, Franklin stood beside the fireplace in the long Privy chamber. For nearly an hour he listened in silence, as accusations tumbled around him. The expression on his face never changed. Somehow he stifled every angry impulse to protest. With remarkable dignity he let Wedderburn's tirade run its course.

In the days that followed, Franklin's enemies renewed their attack through the London papers. They called him "the old veteran of mischief," and "the living emblem of iniquity in gray hair." They dubbed his apartment "Judas' office in Craven Street."

For Franklin, the worst blow was a letter stating that he could no longer serve as Postmaster General of North America. Almost singlehandedly, he had developed the American postal system into a profitable and effective means of communication among the colonies. By removing him from his position as its head, his enemies had stripped him of one of his proudest achievements.

Publicly, Franklin was in disgrace. But his close friends remained loyal, and his social life was still rewarding. He went on with his electrical experiments and with his writing. Though his letters were routinely opened by British officials, he tried to inform the colonies of what was happening in the mother country.

In the fall of 1774, Deborah Franklin told William that she would not live through another winter. If her husband did not return soon, she would never see him again. In December she had a stroke, and she died four days later. A messenger rushed the news to New Jersey, and William rode through a howling blizzard to attend his stepmother's funeral.

Benjamin Franklin and Deborah Read had been married for nearly forty-five years. Yet they had spent fifteen years of that long marriage living apart. Despite their long separations, Franklin always spoke of their partnership as a happy one. Two years before Deborah's death, he wrote to her, "It seems but t'other day since you and I were ranked among the boys and girls, so swiftly does time fly. We have, however, great reason to be thankful that so much of our lives has passed so happily."

At last, after eleven years in England, Franklin set sail for America once more. He arrived in Philadelphia on May 5, 1775. Three weeks before, British soldiers had fired on colonial militia at two villages in Massachusetts, Lexington and

With the Battle of Lexington, the last hope for peace between England and the colonies was gone.

Concord. The last hope for peace was gone. The shots at Lexington and Concord had shattered the fine, noble vase of the British Empire.

At last Benjamin Franklin was ready to take up the cause of independence for America. He was nearly seventy, but he became an ardent revolutionary.

11
"We Must All Hang Together"

Franklin arrived in Philadelphia to find the city preparing for war. At sunrise and sunset, bakers, carpenters, and shopkeepers marched in formation on the public square. Teenage apprentices and farmhands practiced their marksmanship and boasted what they would do when the redcoats came. "The unanimity is amazing," Franklin wrote. He rejoiced that the colonies were finally drawing together for a common cause.

Franklin was full of optimism. He was certain that the colonies could easily shake off British rule. For one thing, they had sheer numbers on their side. "Britain, at the expense of three million [pounds], has killed one hundred fifty yankees this campaign, which is twenty thousand pounds a head," he wrote to his friend Joseph Priestley. "During the same time, sixty thousand children have been born in America."

But thousands of colonists still balked at the notion of independence. Many Americans feared that a break with Britain would lead to short supplies and soaring prices. Others doubted that the colonies could protect themselves from Indians or foreign invaders on their own. And many had a deep, unquestioning loyalty to England. For these loyalists, rebellion against the mother country was unthinkable.

One colonist who remained a loyal British subject was Governor William Franklin of New Jersey. Once William and his father had been as close as brothers or intimate friends. But now their political differences tore them apart. As the colonies readied themselves for war, Franklin accused his son of "[seeing] everything through government eyes."

In 1776, William Franklin was arrested for his loyalist leanings. He was held a prisoner in Connecticut for two years. When his wife, Elizabeth, lay dying, General George Washington turned down his request to go to her bedside.

Some Americans had questioned Benjamin Franklin's loyalty, too, during his long years in England. But his outrageous treatment at the hands of Wedderburn and the Privy Council put any doubts to rest. Franklin was a true American, who had suffered pain and humiliation for his country.

Franklin was one of the revolution's most trusted insiders. He represented Pennsylvania in the Continental Congress, the hastily assembled governing body for the united colonies. The Continental Congress returned him to his office as Postmaster General. As the new government took shape, Franklin improved mail delivery along the Atlantic coast from Maine to Georgia. The system that he created is the direct ancestor of the postal system that serves the United States today.

Benjamin Franklin was also a member of the Committee of Secret Correspondence. The committee was a group of patiots who kept in touch with friends in England and allies all over Europe. Information slipped back and forth across borders in coded messages. Sometimes secrets were written in invisible ink. The intrigues grew so complicated that it was soon hard to know who was spying upon whom.

Despite Franklin's optimism it was soon clear that the war would not be easy to win. The American soldiers were ill-trained and poorly armed. Epidemics of smallpox ravaged the army camps. How could the Americans hope to fight the most powerful nation in the world? They would need all the help they could get.

In the spring of 1776, an American delegation set out to request support from Canada. At seventy, Franklin was by far the oldest member of the party. Sailing up the Hudson, their sloop was battered by a fierce gale. Another storm overtook them as they crossed Lake George by flatboat. There were long days of jolting rides over wilderness roads.

The journey to Canada took nearly a month. By the time he reached Montreal, Franklin was exhausted, and his legs were painfully swollen from gout. Then, as though the trip had not been bad enough, the Canadians refused to help in the war effort. They claimed they were perfectly happy under British rule. The whole expedition came to nothing.

When he finally returned to Philadelphia, Franklin was ill for weeks. Patiently, his daughter Sarah nursed him back to health. He spent many peaceful hours reading and playing with his grandchildren.

But this quiet interlude did not last long. In June, the Continental Congress appointed a committee to draft an official declaration of independence. The committee included John Adams of Massachusetts, Thomas Jefferson of Virginia, and Benjamin Franklin.

The declaration would announce to the world that the former colonies were now a sovereign nation. It had to be written clearly and gracefully. Thomas Jefferson wrote the first draft. He then showed it to Adams and Franklin, who suggested a few changes. Perhaps Franklin's best-known

Franklin, on the left, meeting with the committee to draft the Declaration of Independence.

A draft of the Declaration of Independence in Thomas Jefferson's handwriting. In the first line of the second paragraph, Franklin suggested the change from "sacred and undeniable" to "self-evident."

contribution involved Jefferson's line: "We hold these truths to be sacred and undeniable." Franklin suggested that the sentence should read instead: "We hold these truths to be self-evident."

On July 4, 1776, the Congress voted to accept the Declaration of Independence. Four days later, a cheering crowd gathered before the Pennsylvania State House to hear the document read aloud. Bells pealed, and a bonfire roared on the square. In the excitement, someone tore the British coat of arms from the State House and tossed it onto the flames.

If the rebels won their fight for independence, they would be hailed as heroes and patriots. But if Great Britain stamped out the revolution, its leaders would be condemned as traitors. Treason was a high crime, punishable by death.

This thought must have been in Franklin's mind when he and the other members of the Continental Congress met in August to sign the official copy of the Declaration of Independence. John Hancock of Massachusetts was the first to put his signature on the historic document. According to an often-repeated story, he turned to the others and remarked, "There must be no pulling different ways; we must all hang together." "Yes," Franklin replied, "we must indeed all hang together, or most assuredly we shall all hang separately."

Philadᵃ. July 5. 1775

Mr Strahan,

You are a Member of Parliament, and one of that Majority which has doomed my Country to Destruction. — You have begun to burn our Towns, and murder our People. — Look upon your Hands! — They are stained with the Blood of your Relations! — You and I were long Friends: — You are now my Enemy, — and

I am,

Yours,

B Franklin

A letter from Franklin to a former British friend, William Strahan, written the day after the Declaration of Independence was accepted by the Continental Congress.

12
The Envoy to Paris

Franklin once said that "traveling is one way of lengthening life." In 1776, at the age of seventy, he put this belief to the test. His health was failing, and he grew tired easily. But when the Continental Congress appointed him to serve with the American envoy to Paris, he did not hesitate to say yes.

Canada had refused to support the American war for independence. But the French might prove a valuable ally. France had no love for England. The two nations had gone to war four times since 1700. Perhaps, the Congress reasoned, Franklin and his fellow commissioners could persuade France to help the united colonies.

Franklin crossed the Atlantic on the *Reprisal*, a

war sloop that many considered too battered to make the long voyage. With him sailed two of his grandsons — Sarah's seven-year-old son Benjamin and William's sixteen-year-old son Temple.

The voyage was full of thrills for the two boys. Once a British man-of-war chased the *Reprisal* for miles. Then, off the French coast, the *Reprisal* captured two small English ships. But for Franklin, the trip was exhausting. When he finally came ashore at Auray, France, he could barely stand.

The Reprisal *being chased by a British man-of-war.*

He thoroughly revived on the 250-mile journey overland to Paris. Everywhere his carriage stopped, Franklin was greeted by eager admirers. Scientists and noblemen introduced him to the pleasures of French dining, and discussed philosophy over goblets of the finest wine.

Franklin found Paris a fascinating city of theaters, cathedrals, and formal gardens. But while the French aristocracy lived in splendor, the common people struggled against crushing poverty. They were heavily taxed by the government, and were also obliged to pay tithes to the Catholic Church.

To the French, Franklin was an honest, homespun frontiersman. Instead of a fashionable powdered wig, he sported a fur hat. Although spectacles were shunned by the Paris elite, Franklin wore bifocals — glasses with double lenses, which he had invented himself. Best of all, Franklin's notions about liberty echoed the new ideas that were springing up among the French people. " 'Tis a common observation here that our cause is the cause of all mankind," Franklin wrote in 1777, "and that we are fighting for their liberty in defending our own."

Paris lavished Franklin with attention and praise. His portrait appeared above mantelpieces all over the city. Miniature likenesses decorated the lids of snuffboxes and the handles of pocket knives. Franklin wrote to Sarah that he dared not do anything that would force him to run away,

Ben Franklin, in fur hat and bifocals.

for his face was so well-known that he could never hide.

The face that the French so admired had softened with age. Portraits painted in Paris showed a man of quiet dignity with a warm, kindly smile. Yet the eyes gleam with a hint of mischief. Franklin's life-style in France hardly ranked him as a man of the people. In his house at Passy, a village just outside Paris, he basked in unashamed luxury. Nine servants ran his errands, polished his boots, and cooked his meals. He slept late and lingered over long breakfasts. Morning and evening his house was crowded with visitors — scientists, economists, and French ladies who played for him on the harpsichord and crooned soulful love songs. In February 1779, his cellars contained 1,041 bottles of wine and 48 bottles of rum. Somewhere Franklin had forgotten that he once listed frugality among the virtues he intended to master.

Franklin read French well, but he spoke the language clumsily. Nevertheless, he set out to win French support for the American revolution. He met frequently with the flamboyant courtier and playwright Caron de Beaumarchais, who secretly shipped muskets and powder to the colonists. He encouraged France to open its ports to John Paul Jones, the bold American privateer who had captured dozens of British ships. But diplomacy was painfully slow. France refused to give the Americans full support until it was clear they could

A painting of Marie Antoinette receiving Franklin at the French court, and placing a laurel wreath on his head.

win the war. And it looked as though they could not win the war without full French support.

Almost from the moment Franklin set foot in France, the British were aware of his activities. The British secret service had ways of keeping a close watch on all of his movements. News flowed into London about the comings and goings of "72," as Franklin was called in the coded reports.

Franklin was delighted when Edward Bancroft, an old friend from his London days, turned up in

France. He invited Bancroft to be his long-term houseguest at Passy. Franklin never suspected that Bancroft was listening at keyholes and taking notes on his private conversations. For all his cleverness, he could not imagine that a friend might betray him.

Late in 1777, word reached Paris that the Americans had won a stunning victory over British forces at Saratoga, New York. At last the French felt safe to pledge their support to the rebellious colonies. Franklin helped to draw up a treaty of alliance.

The treaty was signed in a quiet ceremony at the Hotel de Lautrec in Paris. For the occasion, Franklin wore a coat of blue Manchester velvet. One of the other American commissioners asked him why he had chosen that particular coat. "[To have] a little revenge," he replied. "I wore this coat on the day Wedderburn abused me at Whitehall."

Once the French had committed themselves to aid in the war effort, they fought the British on the high seas, and sent shipload after shipload of arms to America. But the struggle dragged on. Sometimes the Continental treasury was so empty that the army went without new boots and survived on short rations. Franklin persuaded the French to lend vast sums of money that kept the American cause afloat.

More than ever, Franklin was troubled by the gout — a condition that caused severe swelling in the joints. Gout was regarded as a disease of the wealthy, since it seemed to be caused by rich food and lack of exercise. At times the pain was so intense that Franklin could barely move. But even in the midst of an agonizing attack, Franklin managed to draw on his sense of humor. In his "Dialogue between Franklin and the Gout" he mocked the lavish life-style that he knew brought on his suffering. "Behold your friend at Auteuil," the Gout chides him in the dialogue. "When she honors you with a visit she comes on foot. . . . But you go to Auteuil in your carriage, though it is not further from Passy to Auteuil than from Auteuil to Passy."

Not everyone was amused by Franklin's life-style. John Adams, who had also been appointed a commissioner to France, complained that Franklin was always entertaining company when he needed to see him on business. "He loves his ease, hates to offend, and seldom gives any opinion until obliged to do so," Adams wrote peevishly. "It is his policy never to say yes or no decidedly." Perhaps Adams was jealous of Franklin's popularity. He himself never won true acceptance in France.

Franklin knew that Adams and others had spoken against him. Perhaps he feared that he would soon be dismissed from his post. In March 1781, he sent the Congress his resignation, explaining that his health no longer permitted him to serve as commissioner. But the Congress still had con-

John Adams, who later became the second president of the United States.

fidence in his abilities. His resignation was denied. Three months later, as the war finally drew to a close, he was appointed to help negotiate the terms of peace with Great Britain.

From the first, Franklin realized it would be no easy task. He commented that "blessed are the peacemakers" might be true in the next world, but in this one they were often cursed.

Franklin and the other commissioners, John Adams and John Jay, agreed that the British must

111

grant full independence to the colonies. In addition, Franklin hoped to expand America's territory by annexing the vast land of Canada to the north. He reasoned that the British should turn over Canada to repay the Americans for the losses they had suffered during the war. The British had confiscated American property, pillaged towns, and encouraged the Indians to raid settlements along the frontier.

In the final peace negotiations, Franklin had to give up on his Canada enterprise. But all in all, he was satisfied with the terms of the treaty, which was signed in 1783. After the brief ceremony, the British and American diplomats dined together at his house in Passy.

In his youth and middle age, Franklin admired England and the mighty British Empire. Now, nearing eighty, he had signed the pact that severed America from Great Britain forever.

13
Home at Last

After the Treaty of Paris was signed, Franklin enjoyed some leisure time at Passy. He devoted himself to his great loves — writing and science. A recent French invention seemed especially promising, and he studied it with his usual enthusiasm. This invention was the hot-air balloon, the answer to mankind's age-old dream of flight. Franklin witnessed some of the first balloon launches in the world and was dazzled by the possibilities. To his enormous delight, he received the first letter carried by balloon across the English Channel.

According to one story, someone asked Franklin what good a hot-air balloon could be. "What good," Franklin retorted, "is a newborn baby?"

A hot air balloon lifting off in September 1784.

In 1785, Congress finally freed Franklin from his diplomatic duties in France. At last, after nine years, he could return to Philadelphia. By now his health was so poor that he seldom left Passy. But he yearned to see his family and friends in America. He determined to make the long voyage across the Atlantic one last time.

Franklin had many close friends in France and had earned the enduring respect of the French people. A great crowd of wellwishers gathered at Passy to see him off. He left the village carried in a royal litter, splendidly cushioned against the jolts of the road.

Ill though he was, Franklin spent the sea voyage making scientific observations. He kept daily records of the temperature of the air and water. He studied the varieties of seaweed and the effects of the Gulf Stream. He wrote long letters to his scientist friends on an improved diet for sailors, and the use of watertight compartments to prevent ships from sinking.

Occasionally he found time to write in his journal. On September 14, 1785, the entry reads: "... A light breeze brought us above Gloucester Point, in full view of dear Philadelphia! ... My son-in-law came with a boat for us; we landed at Market Street wharf, where we were received by a crowd of people with huzzas, and accompanied with acclamations quite to my door. Found my family well. God be praised and thanked for all His mercies!"

If Franklin dreamed of a peaceful retirement, it was not to be. Visitors streamed through the house to welcome him back. The Speaker of the Pennsylvania Assembly, the provost of the Pennsylvania Academy, and members of the state militia all came to congratulate him on a lifetime of achievement. He met with the Union Fire Company, which he had founded almost fifty years earlier. He spoke before the American Philosophical Society.

Franklin had only been home for a month when

he was elected president (or governor) of Pennsylvania. He did not attend many sessions of the assembly, which he found long and dull. But he worked hard from behind the scenes. In 1786 he helped to outlaw whipping, ear-cropping, and branding as punishments for crimes.

In the meantime, the framework of the new American nation was being hammered together. Franklin was dismayed when the bald eagle was chosen as the national emblem. The eagle, he contended, was "a bird of bad moral character." Rather than find its own food, it stole from the smaller fish-hawk. Besides, it was a "rank coward." He argued that the wild turkey was much more respectable. "He is . . . a bird of courage, and would not hesitate to attack a grenadier of the British Guards who should presume to invade his farmyard with a red coat on."

In the spring of 1787, all of the thirteen states, except Rhode Island which refused, selected delegates to attend a convention in Philadelphia. The delegates would construct a set of laws, or constitution, to organize and govern the new nation. At eighty-one Benjamin Franklin was the oldest delegate to the Constitutional Convention.

Public speaking was never Franklin's strong point. Now his voice was feeble with age, and he could not stand up long enough to address a meeting. To deliver speeches before the Constitutional Convention, he wrote out his remarks and had them read aloud for him.

Franklin brought a number of controversial ideas to the Constitutional Convention. He wanted to see a unicameral, or one-house, congress. He also suggested that two people should share the presidency, to prevent a single individual from becoming too powerful. Neither of these ideas was accepted. We now have a single president and a two-house congress.

Franklin's greatest contribution to the Consti-

The signing of the United States Constitution, in 1787. Ben Franklin is on the left.

tutional Convention was his gift for diplomacy. He had a remarkable knack for working out compromises between warring factions. When the delegates were hopelessly tangled in debate, he could point out the goals they had in common. Furthermore, his sense of humor brightened many dull moments in the long, complex proceedings.

After four months of study and discussion, gentle persuasion and fierce debate, the delegates finally approved the Constitution of the United States. During the formal signing on September 17, 1787, Franklin pointed to the image of the sun painted on the back of George Washington's chair. He had looked at it many times throughout the convention, trying to decide whether it was rising or setting. "Now," he told the delegates standing near him, "I have the happiness to know that it is a rising and not a setting sun."

The Constitution was one of the great documents in the history of democracy. Yet it made no attempt to bring an end to slavery. In the past Franklin had owned slaves, and he had arranged for the sale of slaves through his shop on Market Street. But over the years he had come to believe that slavery was morally wrong. In 1787 he threw his support behind the antislavery movement when he became president of the Pennsylvania Society for the Promotion of the Abolition of Slavery and the Relief of Free Negroes Unlawfully Held in Bondage.

THE CONSTITUTION

OF THE

PENNSYLVANIA SOCIETY,

FOR PROMOTING THE

ABOLITION OF SLAVERY,

AND THE RELIEF OF

FREE NEGROES,

UNLAWFULLY HELD IN

BONDAGE.

BEGUN IN THE YEAR 1774, AND ENLARGED ON THE
TWENTY-THIRD OF APRIL, 1787.

TO WHICH ARE ADDED,

THE ACTS OF

The General Aſſembly of Pennſylvania,

FOR THE GRADUAL

ABOLITION OF SLAVERY.

*" All Things whatſoever ye would that Men ſhould do to you,
do ye even ſo to them ; for this is the Law and the Pro-
phets."* Matth. vii. 12.

PHILADELPHIA:
PRINTED BY FRANCIS BAILEY, FOR " THE PENNSYLVANIA
SOCIETY FOR PROMOTING THE ABOLITION OF SLA-
VERY, AND THE RELIEF OF FREE NEGROES
UNLAWFULLY HELD IN BONDAGE."
M,DCC,LXXXVIII.

The constitution of the Pennsylvania Society for Promoting the Abolition of Slavery, and the Relief of Free Negroes, Unlawfully held in Bondage.

Franklin served as president of Pennsylvania until October 1788. He never ran for public office again. In his retirement, he spent much of his time writing letters. His warm, lively correspondence kept him close to old friends in England and France and throughout the new United States.

The summer after he retired from public life, Franklin drew up his last will and testament. He divided his estate generously between Sarah and her husband, and his grandsons Benjamin Bache and Temple Franklin. He left money to his sister Jane Mecom, and to numerous relatives in Boston. There was a bequest to the Pennsylvania Hospital, which he had helped to establish. He left money to the free schools of Boston, to be used for a special annual award for students of high merit. To this day, the Franklin Awards are still granted each year at the Boston Latin School.

Franklin's most extraordinary bequest was a trust fund for the cities of Boston and Philadelphia. He asked that money from the fund be given each year to help promising young tradesmen make a start in life. The bulk of the money would be invested and used over the next two centuries for education and other programs to benefit the public.

Even in his will, however, Franklin remained bitter toward his son William. They never regained their old closeness after the war was over. Franklin left William some land in Nova Scotia, a collection of books and papers, and the debts William had run up while being supported by his father. "The part he acted against me in the late war," Franklin wrote, "will account for my leaving him no more of an estate [which] he endeavored to deprive me of."

Franklin still suffered from gout. Even worse, he had a condition that doctors diagnosed as a stone in the bladder. Often he could not leave his bed and resorted to opium to control the pain. Nevertheless, he completed the autobiography that he had begun in England eighteen years earlier. When he was too ill to sit up, he dictated his work to his devoted grandson Benjamin.

"In this world, nothing can be said to be certain except death and taxes," Franklin wrote in the last year of his life. He was witnessing the dawn of an especially uncertain age. As a fledgling nation, the United States struggled to resolve daunting problems. In France, a bloody revolution had broken out, and Franklin worried over the safety of dear friends in Paris. The whole world, it seemed, was changing. He could do little now to affect the course those changes would take. The time had come for him to stand back while others mapped out the road ahead.

Franklin's pain was unrelenting. His once stocky body grew shrunken and frail. Yet he remained cheerful to his family and friends, and never lost interest in the world around him. He read the newspapers carefully every day. He delighted in Sarah's new baby, "a little good-natured girl whom I begin to love as well as the rest." Every afternoon his nine-year-old grand-daugher, Deborah Bache, sat beside him while she did her homework. "For my own personal ease, I should have died two years ago," he wrote to President George Washington, "but, though these years have been spent in excruciating pain, I am pleased that I have lived them."

Franklin's condition grew steadily worse. At last he passed into a coma. With his grandsons Benjamin and Temple watching at his bedside, he died on the night of April 17, 1790. He was eighty-four years old.

A black-bordered edition of the *Pennsylvania Gazette* announced Franklin's death. Bells tolled, and flags hung at half mast. On April 21, a funeral procession assembled in front of the State House. All of the city's dignitaries were there. The ministers of every church, the leading bankers, lawyers, physicians, and businessmen, judges, printers, and educators joined Franklin's family and friends on the solemn walk to the Christ Church Burying Ground. Never before in the history of America had so many people gathered for a funeral — some 20,000 mourners in all.

Franklin was laid to rest beside his wife, Deborah. The inscription on his headstone reads simply: "Benjamin and Deborah Franklin, 1790." But more than sixty years earlier, when he was only twenty-three, Franklin had written an epi-

Epitaph written 1728.

The Body of
B Franklin Printer,
(Like the Cover of an old Book
Its Contents torn out
And stript of its Lettering & Gilding)
Lies here, Food for Worms.
But the Work shall not be lost;
For it will, (as he believ'd) appear once more,
In a new and more elegant Edition
Revised and corrected,
By the Author.

Franklin's handwritten epitaph, humorously using the terms of his trade.

taph for himself that captures his philosophical
view of life, even as a young man:

THE BODY
OF
B. FRANKLIN
PRINTER
(LIKE THE COVER OF AN OLD BOOK,
ITS CONTENTS TORN OUT
AND STRIPT OF ITS LETTERING AND GILDING),
LIES HERE, FOOD FOR WORMS.
BUT THE WORK SHALL NOT BE LOST,
FOR IT WILL (AS HE BELIEVED) APPEAR ONCE MORE
IN A NEW AND MORE ELEGANT EDITION
REVISED AND CORRECTED
BY
THE AUTHOR

Index

SCHOLASTIC BIOGRAPHY

APPLE® PAPERBACKS

Pick an Apple and Polish Off Some Great Reading!

BEST-SELLING APPLE TITLES